Yo Mama So Dumb Jokes

Jokes So Funny Yo Mama Would Laugh Too

Published by Glowworm Press
7 Nuffield Way
Abingdon OX14 1RL
By Charlie Crapper

Yo Mama So Dumb

These yo mama so dumb jokes will have you laughing out loud. These yo mama jokes are so funny yo mama would laugh too.

We hope you enjoy these yo mama so dumb gags, which we can confidently say is the largest selection of yo mama so dumb and you mama so stupid jokes ever assembled in one place. Jam packed full of the very best kid friendly yo mama so stupid jokes; this book will have you in stitches.

Copyright Glowworm Press
All Rights Reserved. No part of this publication may be reproduced in any form or by any means without the written permission of the publisher Glowworm Press; with the exception of reviews for a magazine, newspaper, blog or website. Product names referred to within this publication are the property of their respective trademark holders. This book is not authorised or endorsed by the aforementioned interests. This book is licensed for your personal enjoyment only.

As you read through this ultimate collection of Yo Mama So Dumb jokes – 250 of them – try and pick out your favorite. It will be hard, as there are just so many to choose from.

Enjoy!

Yo mama so dumb she shut herself in the fridge to see if the light really goes off.

Yo mama so dumb her eyes lit up when I shone a flashlight in her ears.

Yo mama so dumb she put her iPad in a blender because she wanted to make apple juice.

Yo mama so dumb when laptop froze she stuck it in the microwave.

Yo mama so dumb she went to Taco Bell to pay her phone bill.

Yo mama so dumb she ordered her sushi well done.

Yo mama so dumb she burnt her ear doing the ironing when the phone rang.

Yo mama so dumb she put on a coat to chew winter fresh gum.

Yo mama so dumb she took a pencil to the bedroom because she wanted to draw the curtains.

Yo mama so dumb she ran outside with her purse because she heard there was a change in the weather.

Yo mama so dumb when she saw a Wrong Way sign in her rear-view mirror, she turned around.

Yo mama so dumb you can't tell her knock knock jokes as she will go open the door.

Yo mama so dumb she sold the house to pay the mortgage.

Yo mama so dumb she thinks a stereotype is a car radio.

Yo mama so dumb she thought a law suit was something you wear to court.

Yo mama so dumb she thinks deadbeat is a type of music.

Yo mama so dumb she put on anti-bug spray before going to the flea market.

Yo mama so dumb she put on glasses to watch 20/20.

Yo mama so dumb she went to the aquarium to buy a Blu-Ray.

Yo mama so dumb when I told her I was reading a book by Homer, she asked if I had anything by Bart or Lisa.

Yo mama so dumb she needs twice as much sense to be a half-wit.

Yo mama so dumb she thought brownies points were coupons for a bake sale.

Yo mama so dumb she was on a street corner with a sign saying "Will eat for food."

Yo mama so dumb she uses Old Spice for cooking.

Yo mama so dumb she climbed over a glass wall to see what was behind it.

Yo mama so dumb if you gave her a penny for her thoughts, you'd get change.

Yo mama so dumb she got hit by a cup and told the police she got mugged.

Yo mama so dumb she put a watch in the piggy bank and said she was saving time.

Yo mama so dumb when she threw a grenade at me, I pulled the pin and threw it back.

Yo mama so dumb she got locked in Mattress World and slept on the floor.

Yo mama so dumb it takes her a week to get rid of a 24 hour virus.

Yo mama so dumb she threw a rock at the ground and missed.

Yo mama so dumb she laughs at her husband cos he as an ugly wife.

Yo mama so dumb the Psychic Friends read her mind and gave her her money back

Yo mama so dumb she used a real mouse to use the computer.

Yo mama so dumb she can't tell her family from her enemies.

Yo mama so dumb she drives her car with the handbrake on.

Yo mama so dumb she combs the hair in her nose and not on her head.

Yo mama so dumb she bought a used ring that has never been worn.

Yo mama so dumb she asked you "What is the number for 911".

Yo mama so dumb when she read on her job application to not write below the dotted line she put "O.K."

Yo mama so dumb she tried to hang dumb bells on her Christmas tree.

Yo mama so dumb she bought a video camera to record cable TV shows at home.

Yo mama so dumb that under "Education" on her job application, she put "Hooked on Phonics."

Yo mama so dumb she put out the cigarette butt that was heating your house.

Yo mama so dumb she watches "The Three Stooges" and takes notes.

Yo mama so dumb she was born on Independence Day and can't remember her birthday.

Yo mama so dumb she thought gangrene was a golf course.

Yo mama so dumb she tried to read an audio book.

Yo mama so dumb it takes her a month to get rid of the 7 day itch.

Yo mama so dumb she thought the Nazis were saying "Hi! Hitler"

Yo mama so dumb she asked me what kind of jeans I had on and I said "Guess" so she said "Levi's".

Yo mama so dumb she looked at a recipe book that told her to separate an egg from the white so she left the yolk in the kitchen and put the white in the living room.

Yo mama so dumb she thinks Fleetwood Mac is a new hamburger at McDonalds.

Yo mama so dumb she thought a runny nose was an exercise.

Yo mama so dumb she went to take the 44 bus but took the 22 twice instead.

Yo mama so dumb she jumped off a cliff so she can fly with the birds.

Yo mama so dumb she rented a hot air balloon so she can watch men play Air Hockey.

Yo mama so dumb she went into the YMCA thinking it was Macy's.

Yo mama so dumb I saw her going into a Subway restaurant asking people if she was late

Yo mama so dumb when she had "chill for 1 hour" in her recipe, she left the kitchen, sat down and watched TV.

Yo mama so dumb when she saw a "50% OFF" sign she went looking for the other half.

Yo mama so dumb she took a ruler to bed to see how long she slept.

Yo mama so dumb when I rang the doorbell she checked the microwave.

Yo mama so dumb when the doctor told her to burn some calories she set her fat ass on fire.

Yo mama so dumb she threw the clock out the window to see time fly.

Yo mama so dumb when I said one man's trash is another man's treasure she jumped in a trash bin.

Yo mama so dumb she thought asphalt was a butt disorder.

Yo mama so dumb when she saw a nickel back gorilla she gave it five cents.

Yo mama so dumb when asked what the capital of California was she answered "C".

Yo mama so dumb when she went to court when the judge said "Order in court" she said burger and fries.

Yo mama so dumb she tried to use Monopoly money at the grocery store.

Yo mama so dumb when the Cop pulled her over and gave her a ticket she said "What movie are we going to see?"

Yo mama so dumb she heard about the Rolling Stones and went out to the mountains and stated searching for them.

Yo mama so dumb she thought Nickelback was a refund.

Yo mama so dumb she goes to a White Castle, flushes the toilet and calls it a royal flush.

Yo mama so dumb when I told her she needed to take a drug test, she said "Great, which one are we gonna try first?"

Yo mama so dumb she thought a Jolly Rancher was a gay cowboy.

Yo mama so dumb she got hit by a cup and told the police she got mugged.

Yo mama so dumb not even Google could translate her.

Yo mama so dumb it takes her a day to cook a 3 minutes egg.

Yo mama so dumb she tried to climb Mountain Dew.

Yo mama so dumb she booked an appointment with Dr Pepper after she fell off Mountain Dew.

Yo mama so dumb she sprayed a tree with axe body spray and thought it would fall down.

Yo mama so dumb she bought tickets to Xbox Live.

Yo mama so dumb when she had to leave a voicemail she walked to my house and screamed in my mailbox.

Yo mama so dumb she thinks menopause is a button on a DVD player.

Yo mama so dumb she goes to the Apple store to get a Big Mac meal.

Yo mama so dumb she thinks that Harlem Shake is a drink.

Yo mama so dumb she thought Spotify was a stain remover.

Yo mama so dumb she went to the eye doctor to buy an iPad.

Yo mama so dumb when I said drinks is on the house she went to get a ladder.

Yo mama so dumb when the smoke alarm turned off, she tried to turn it back on by starting a fire.

Yo mama so dumb she brought a bible to Church's Chicken.

Yo mama so dumb that she put a battery in water to make an energy drink.

Yo mama so dumb she put two M&M's in her ears and thought she was listening to Eminem.

Yo mama so dumb she took her dog to Pet Smart to get an IQ Test.

Yo mama so dumb she went to the dentist to get her Bluetooth fixed.

Yo mama so dumb she made an appointment with Diet Dr. Pepper to get thinner.

Yo mama so dumb she brought a ladder to go to High school.

Yo mama so dumb when I said "That act is stealing the show", she called the Police.

Yo mama so dumb she thinks gluteus maximus is a Roman emperor.

Yo mama so dumb she looked in the mirror and said what you looking at.

Yo mama so dumb she put sugar on her pillow because she wanted sweet dreams.

Yo mama so dumb she thought Dunkin Donuts was a basketball team.

Yo mama so dumb she put a watch in the piggy bank and said she was saving time.

Yo mama so dumb when I said check out this new website she got a broom and said "Where's the spider?"

Yo mama so dumb when I said Christmas was around the corner she went looking for it.

Yo mama so dumb she went to the library to find Facebook.

Yo mama so dumb she's living proof that humans can live without a brain.

Yo mama so dumb Willy Wonka couldn't sugar coat it.

Yo mama so dumb when I asked her if she knew Pharell from the Neptunes she said she only knows people from Earth.

Yo mama so dumb when the cop pulled her over and gave her a ticket she said "What movie are we going to see?"

Yo mama so dumb she thinks Christmas Wrap is Snoop Dogg's holiday album.

Yo mama so dumb that she thought Boyz II Men was a day care center.

Yo mama so dumb she got hit by a punchline.

Yo mama so dumb she took an umbrella to see Purple Rain.

Yo mama so dumb it took her 2 hours to watch 60 minutes.

Yo mama so dumb she talks into an envelope to send a voicemail.

Yo mama so dumb when it was chilly outside, she ran outside with a spoon.

Yo mama so dumb you have to dig for her IQ.

Yo mama so dumb she told everyone that she was illegitimate because she couldn't read.

Yo mama so dumb she puts lipstick on her head just to make-up her mind.

Yo mama so dumb she threw water at the computer to put out a flame war.

Ok, that's halfway through now - we hope you're enjoying this book.

It might be a good idea to have a breather from all these jokes - there are just too many to take in one go.

It can be hard when there are some many great jokes, but do remember to decide which is your favorite.

Ready? OK let's get onto the second half – another 125 jokes to come!

Yo mama so dumb she thinks that a scholarship is a boat full of students.

Yo mama so dumb she went to the beach to surf the internet.

Yo mama so dumb she called me, then asked for my phone number.

Yo mama so dumb she brought a six pack of Budweiser with her to school, hoping she could make her son Bud Wiser.

Yo mama so dumb she put her iPad in the blender because she said that she wanted to make apple juice.

Yo mama so dumb that when she got sick she went to the shoe store to find "Doc Martens".

Yo mama so dumb her IQ test result came back negative.

Yo mama so dumb she tears apart computers looking for cookies.

Yo mama so dumb when she went for summer school and they asked her to count 1 to 40, she counted 1 2 40.

Yo mama so dumb she thought chicken strips was a strip club for chickens.

Yo mama so dumb she brought her baby girl to a baby shower and left her.

Yo mama so dumb she went to pet store to buy some bird seed, then asked the cashier how long does it take for the birds to grow.

Yo mama so dumb she thought The Exorcist was a workout video.

Yo mama so dumb she sold her car for gasoline money.

Yo mama so dumb the only letters in the alphabet she knows are K.F.C.

Yo mama so dumb she wouldn't buy a game boy because she was a girl.

Yo mama so dumb she tried to download WhatsApp on a public phone.

Yo mama so dumb she bought a solar-powered flashlight.

Yo mama so dumb she thought a tsunami was a kind of Japanese sushi.

Yo mama so dumb she thinks a quarterback is a refund.

Yo mama so dumb her ancestors didn't even think about making fire.

Yo mama so dumb she fell UP a flight of stairs.

Yo mama so dumb she sat on the TV and watched the couch.

Yo mama so dumb she went to a Clippers game for a haircut.

Yo mama so dumb she sold the car for gas money.

Yo mama so dumb she took a ruler to bed to see how long she slept.

Yo mama so dumb I asked her what she does for a living and she said breathe.

Yo mama so dumb she makes Beavis and Butt-Head look like Nobel Prize winners.

Yo mama so dumb she thought she needed a token to get on Soul Train.

Yo mama so dumb she sent me a fax with a stamp on it.

Yo mama so dumb she tried to schedule a physical with Dr. Pepper.

Yo mama so dumb if you knocked on her forehead you would hear an echo.

Yo mama so dumb she thought Fruit Punch was a gay boxer.

Yo mama so dumb when her friend got injured on her left side she thought she was alright.

Yo mama so dumb she thought Meow Mix was a record for cats.

Yo mama so dumb she filled her car with water so she can drive in the Car Pool lane.

Yo mama so dumb when she studied pi in school, she brought a plate to class.

Yo mama so dumb she tripped over a cordless phone.

Yo mama so dumb she hired a blind man for look-out duty.

Yo mama so dumb she threw cats out the window when you said "We need cat litter."

Yo mama so dumb I told her I was dying of laughter and she took me to the hospital.

Yo mama so dumb that calling her dumb would be an insult to dumb people.

Yo mama so dumb she studied for a drug test by taking all of the drugs.

Yo mama so dumb she got her fingers stuck in a website.

Yo mama so dumb she told me everything she knows during a commercial break.

Yo mama so dumb that if I need a brain transplant I'll take hers, because it's barely been used.

Yo mama so dumb if you stand close enough to her you can hear the ocean.

Yo mama so dumb I asked her why she was jumping up and down and she said she taken her medicine and forgotten to shake the bottle.

Yo mama so dumb the government banned her from home schooling her kids.

Yo mama so dumb she thought Starbucks was a bank.

Yo mama so dumb she spent 20 minutes looking at the orange juice box because it said "concentrate".

Yo mama so dumb she took a spoon to the Superbowl.

Yo mama so dumb that after searching for her wedding ring for three days, she realized she was divorced.

Yo mama so dumb when playing Monopoly, before passing go, she stopped and looked both ways.

Yo mama so dumb she told me to meet her at the corner of "WALK" and "DON'T WALK".

Yo mama so dumb when she heard there was a serial killer on the loose she put Captain Crunch in the closet and said I will protect you.

Yo mama so dumb when I told her to go away, she said "Which way?".

Yo mama so dumb she got locked in a grocery store and starved to death.

Yo mama so dumb she tried to hotwire a trolley.

Yo mama so dumb when she saw a stop sign she never moved again.

Yo mama so dumb at the bottom of the application where it says "sign here" she wrote down "Aquarius".

Yo mama so dumb she asked for a price check at the Dollar Store.

Yo mama so dumb if she spoke her mind, she'd probably be speechless.

Yo mama so dumb she studied for a blood test and failed.

Yo mama so dumb she put paper on the TV and called it paper view.

Yo mama so dumb when she heard that 90% of all crimes occur around the home, she moved

Yo mama so dumb when she went to Disneyland she saw a sign that said "Disneyland Left" so she turned around and went home.

Yo mama so dumb she took the Pepsi challenge and chose Dr Pepper.

Yo mama so dumb she couldn't see the forest cause "the trees were blocking it."

Yo mama so dumb she ordered a cheeseburger from McDonald's and said, "Hold the cheese".

Yo mama so dumb she thought Hamburger Helper came with another person.

Yo mama so dumb she thinks socialism means partying.

Yo mama so dumb she had to study all night to pass a urine test.

Yo mama so dumb she thought Tiger Woods was a forest in India.

Yo mama so dumb she tried to drown a fish.

Yo mama so dumb when I was drowning and yelled for a life saver, she said, "Cherry or Grape?"

Yo mama so dumb when the computer said "Press any key to continue", she couldn't find the "Any" key.

Yo mama so dumb she threw a bird off a cliff.

Yo mama so dumb she goes to the frozen food section of the store with a fishing rod.

Yo mama so dumb she took a doughnut back because it had a hole in it.

Yo mama so dumb she bought curtains for her computer because it had Windows.

Yo mama so dumb her shoes say TGIF – toes go in front.

Yo mama so dumb she bought a Ford from the dealership and sat in it for two days because it said focus.

Yo mama so dumb when she shivers you can hear a rattling coming from her head.

Yo mama so dumb she cut holes in her umbrella to see if it was raining.

Yo mama so dumb she tried to pull a root beer out of the ground.

Yo mama so dumb she put dumbbells in a basket and thought she was pushing weight.

Yo mama so dumb when she went to Hollywood, to see the stars, she took a telescope with her.

Yo mama so dumb she went outside to look at the stars and thought it was pokey dots.

Yo mama so dumb I asked her what time she was leaving, she started talking to her watch.

Yo mama so dumb I told her it was raining cats and dogs, she got out a net.

Yo mama so dumb that she thought seaweed was something that fish smoked.

Yo mama so dumb I told her to buy a color TV and she said "What Color?"

Yo mama so dumb she sold her refrigerator to buy groceries.

Yo mama so dumb she tripped over a wireless network.

Yo mama so dumb I asked her how old she is, but she can't count that high.

Yo mama so dumb she put a quarter in a parking meter and waited for a gum ball to come out.

Yo mama so dumb she stepped into a Walgreens and thought the walls were actually supposed to be green

Yo mama so dumb she sat on memory foam and she forgot.

Yo mama so dumb when I asked her for water she said what's the ingredients?

Yo mama so dumb she put two quarters in her ears and said she was listening to 50 cent.

Yo mama so dumb she fell off a boat and couldn't find the water.

Yo mama so dumb that she thinks Justin Bieber is a real beaver.

Yo mama so dumb she thought Snoop Dogg was a real dog.

Yo mama so dumb she thought pumpernickel was a refund.

Yo mama so dumb she thought a lightsaber had less calories.

Yo mama so dumb that when she turned on the TV it was pitch black and she said "I like this show".

Yo mama so dumb when I told her that her birthday was just around the corner she went looking for it.

Yo mama so dumb she stays up all night trying to catch some sleep.

Yo mama so dumb she thought jalapeno poppers were something used to blow up jalapenos

Yo mama so dumb she went to New Delhi in India thinking it was a grand opening of a meat shop.

Yo mama so dumb she went to McDonalds, got a hamburger, put a crown on it, and said Burger King.

Yo mama so dumb when they ask her when was she born she said in the beginning.

Yo mama so dumb she thought the internet was something you catch butterflies with.

Yo mama so dumb she went to Babies R Us and asked where the babies were.

Yo mama so dumb she thought a civil war is a war against manners.

Yo mama so dumb she bought tickets to Xbox Live.

Yo mama so dumb when she plays pool she puts her bathing suit on.

Yo mama so dumb she brought nuts to a Nutcracker.

Yo mama so dumb when she drank "Smart Water" she thought she was going to Harvard.

Yo mama so dumb she stole free samples.

Yo mama so dumb so she took her Barbie dolls to get plastic surgery.

Yo mama so dumb her IQ is the same as her shoe size.

Yo mama so dumb she returned a puzzle because she thought it was broken.

Yo mama so dumb she got hit by a parked car.

Yo mama so dumb her computer mouse was broken so she took it to the vet.

Yo mama so dumb she got awarded the Nobel prize for dumbity.

Wow – that was great fun – and lots of laughs

If you enjoyed it, you can search for our other books on Amazon - Yo Mama So Ugly and Yo Mama So Fat.

Also can whoever bought this book please leave a review on Amazon telling everyone what your favorite joke was that would be great and much appreciated.

Have a great day!

Made in the USA
Las Vegas, NV
16 December 2021